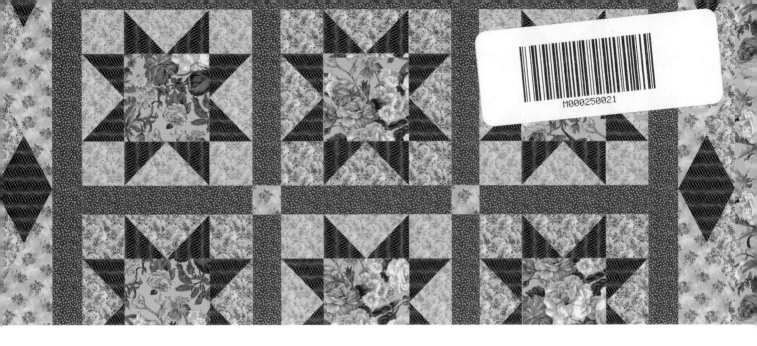

The Sawtooth Star Block

A Classic For Today's Quilts

Building Blocks Series 1 — Book 8

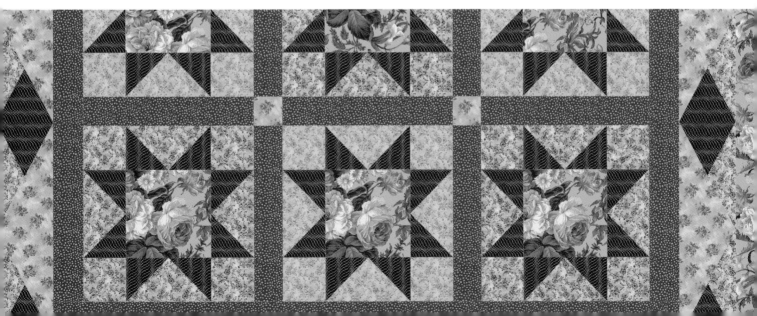

Special thanks to the following
for the beautiful fabrics used
in the quilts in this book:

Fabri-Quilt
Marcus Fabrics
Northcott
Quilting Treasures
Red Rooster Fabrics

All quilt designs by Sandy Boobar and
Sue Harvey of Pine Tree Country Quilts,
www.pinetreecountryquilts.com.

Published by

All American Crafts, Inc.
7 Waterloo Road
Stanhope, NJ 07874
www.allamericancrafts.com

Publisher | **Jerry Cohen**

Chief Executive Officer | **Darren Cohen**

Product Development
Director | **Brett Cohen**

Editor | **Sue Harvey**

Proofreader | **Natalie Rhinesmith**

Art Director | **Kelly Albertson**

Illustrations | **Kathleen Geary, Roni Palmisano
& Chrissy Scholz**

Product Development
Manager | **Pamela Mostek**

Vice President/Quilting Advertising
& Marketing | **Carol Newman**

Printed in China
ISBN: 978-1-936708-04-8
UPC: 793573035271

www.allamericancrafts.com

Contents
Table of Contents

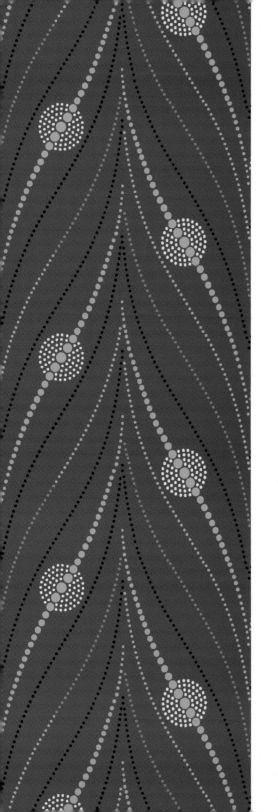

Welcome

Welcome to the Building Blocks series of quilting books.

Whether you're making your first or your one hundred and first quilt, the eight books in this series will be an invaluable addition to your quilting library. Besides featuring the instructions to make a different traditional and timeless block in each book, we've also included charts to give you all the quick information you need to change the block size for your own project.

Each book features complete instructions for three different quilts using the featured block with variations in size, color, and style—all designed to inspire you to use these timeless blocks for quilts with today's look.

The Finishing Basics section in each book gives you the tips and techniques you'll need to border, quilt, and bind the quilts in this book (or any quilt you may choose to make). If you're an experienced quilter, these books will be an excellent addition to your reference library. When you want to enlarge or reduce a block, the numbers are already there for you! No math required!

The blocks in the Building Blocks series of books have stood the test of time and are still favorites with quilters today. Although they're traditional blocks, they look very contemporary in today's bold and beautiful fabrics. This definitely puts them in the category of quilting classics!

For each block, you'll find a little background about its name, origin, or era, just to add a touch of quilting trivia. The block presented in this book is Sawtooth Star. Quilt historian Barbara Brackman notes that its first publication was in 1884 under the name Sawtooth. The addition of Star to its name did not come for almost 100 years—in the late 1970s.

Simple changes in value placement can change one traditional block into another traditional block. The Sawtooth Star block has dark star points, a medium center square, and light outer edge pieces. Switch to dark points and center and light outer edges to make Square and Points. The same block with dark corners, light side edges, and medium points and center becomes Austin. Dark outer edges and light points and center make Evening Star.

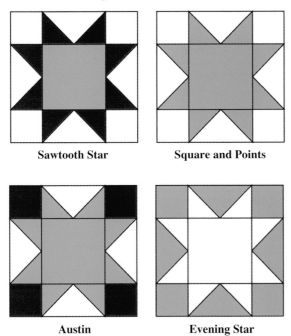

Sawtooth Star   **Square and Points**

Austin   **Evening Star**

In this book, *Framed Stars* and *Scene Through a Telescope* stick with the traditional value placement for this block, whereas *Dressed to the Nines* escapes from tradition into a block that defies all names with its dark center and outer edges. Have fun playing with color and value in the pieces of Sawtooth Star—there is a whole galaxy of new stars waiting for you!

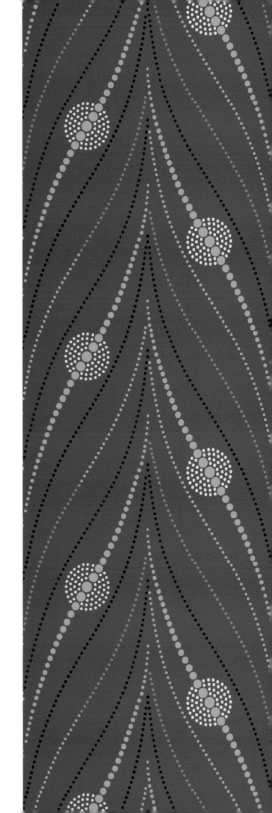

BUILDING THE BLOCK
Use a 1/4" seam allowance throughout.

1. Mark a diagonal line on the wrong side of each C square.

2. Place a marked C square right sides together on the left end of a B rectangle. Stitch on the marked line. Trim the seam allowance to 1/4". Press the C corner to the right side.

3. Place a marked C square right sides together on the right end of the same unit. Stitch on the marked line. Trim the seam allowance to 1/4". Press the C corner to the right side to complete one BC unit.

6

Make 4

Sawtooth Star

Use these instructions to make the blocks for the quilts in this book. The materials needed for each quilt and the cutting instructions are given with the pattern for the quilt. Also included is a Build It Your Way chart with four different sizes for this block and the sizes to cut the pieces for one block. Use this information to design your own quilt or to change the size of any of the quilts in this book.

4. Repeat steps 2 and 3 to complete four BC units total.

5. Sew a BC unit to opposite sides of an A square. Press seams toward the A square. Sew a D square to each end of the two remaining BC units. Press seams toward the D squares. Sew the pieced strips together to complete the block. Press seams away from the center strip.

6. Repeat to complete the number of blocks needed for the quilt that you have chosen.

Build It Better

Stop! Don't mark all those diagonal lines—try this handy technique instead. Draw a straight line perpendicular to the edge of a 3" x 8" piece of paper or template plastic. Place the paper/plastic piece on the bed of your sewing machine with the needle in a straight line with the line on the paper/plastic. Tape the paper/plastic piece to your sewing machine. Place the layered C square/B rectangle on the paper/plastic piece with one corner of C at the edge of the needle and the opposite corner on the marked line on the paper/plastic piece. As you stitch, move the corner of C along the marked line. This puts your stitches exactly along the diagonal of the C square, right where they're supposed to be!

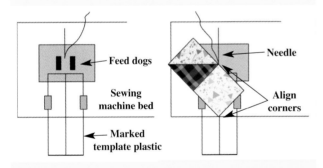

Build It Better

Need a quick gift or decorating idea? Make four 12" blocks. Cut (4) 6½" x 12½" strips from a coordinating fabric. Sew a strip to one edge of each block to complete four placemat tops. Layer the tops with batting and backing, quilt them, and add binding (see Finishing Basics on page 26). Go a step further and make matching napkins: Cut (4) 18½" squares of coordinating fabric. Turn the edges under ¼" and press. Turn them under ¼" again and press. Topstitch all around to finish four napkins.

Build It Your Way

Piece	6" Block	8" Block	12" Block	16" Block
A	3¹/₂" x 3¹/₂"	4¹/₂" x 4¹/₂"	6¹/₂" x 6¹/₂"	8¹/₂" x 8¹/₂"
B	2" x 3¹/₂"	2¹/₂" x 4¹/₂"	3¹/₂" x 6¹/₂"	4¹/₂" x 8¹/₂"
C	2" x 2"	2¹/₂" x 2¹/₂"	3¹/₂" x 3¹/₂"	4¹/₂" x 4¹/₂"
D	2" x 2"	2¹/₂" x 2¹/₂"	3¹/₂" x 3¹/₂"	4¹/₂" x 4¹/₂"

Dressed to the Nines

Dress up a table, a wall, the back of a sofa, or the center of a bed. If you love the new fabrics every season, but hate to invest the time and money in a bed-size quilt, make smaller accents to switch out as your mood changes!

Finished Quilt Size: 48" x 48"
Finished Block Size: 8" x 8"
Number of Blocks: 13
Skill Level: Confident Beginner

MATERIALS
All yardages are based on 42"-wide fabric.

❖ 1 yard of navy floral
❖ 7/8 yard of diagonal plaid
❖ 3/4 yard of white print
❖ 1 yard of medium blue print
❖ 1/2 yard of green dot
❖ 31/4 yards of backing fabric
❖ 56" x 56" piece of batting
❖ Thread to match fabrics
❖ Rotary cutting tools
❖ Basic sewing supplies

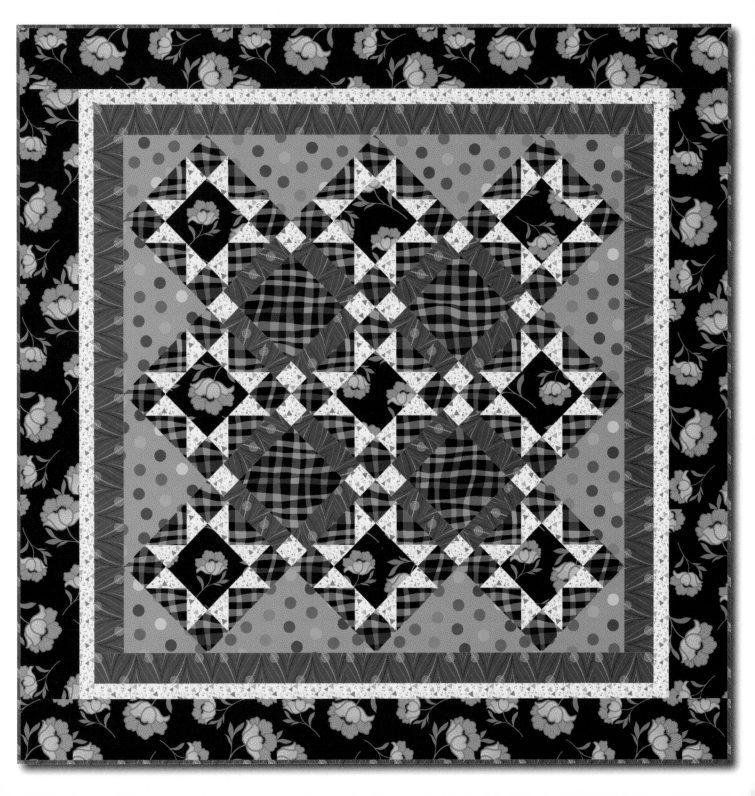

CUTTING

Label all pieces with the letters assigned. They will be used throughout the instructions.

From the navy floral, cut

- 1 strip 4½" x 42"; recut into (9) 4½" A squares
- 5 strips 4½" x 42" for outer border

From the diagonal plaid, cut

- 7 strips 2½" x 42"; recut into (36) 2½" x 4½" B rectangles and (36) 2½" D squares
- 1 strip 5½" x 42"; recut into (4) 5½" E squares

From the white print, cut

- 5 strips 2½" x 42"; recut into (72) 2½" C squares
- 1 strip 2" x 42"; recut into (16) 2" G squares
- 4 strips 1½" x 42" for outer border

From the medium blue print, cut

- 3 strips 2" x 42"; recut into (16) 2" x 5½" F rectangles
- 4 strips 2½" x 42" for inner border
- 5 strips 2¼" x 42" for binding

From the green dot, cut

- 1 strip 12⅝" x 42"; recut into (2) 12⅝" H squares and (2) 6½" I squares, then cut the H squares twice diagonally to make 8 H triangles and the I squares in half diagonally to make 4 I triangles

From the backing fabric, cut

- 2 pieces 56" long

MAKING THE SAWTOOTH STAR BLOCKS

Use a ¼" seam allowance throughout unless otherwise instructed.

1. Refer to Building the Block on page 6 to make nine 8½" x 8½" Sawtooth Star blocks.

Make 9

MAKING THE NINE-PATCH VARIATION BLOCKS

1. Sew a medium blue F rectangle to opposite sides of a plaid E square. Press seams toward the E square.

Make 1

2. Stitch a white G square to each end of a medium blue F rectangle. Press seams toward the G squares. Repeat to make a second pieced strip.

Make 2

3. Sew the pieced strips together to complete one 8½" x 8½" Nine-Patch Variation block. Press seams toward the FG strips.

Make 4

4. Repeat steps 1-3 to complete four blocks total.

COMPLETING THE QUILT CENTER

1. Join the blocks and green dot H triangles in five diagonal rows. Press seams away from the Sawtooth Star blocks. (Refer to the Quilt Assembly Diagram on page 12.)

2. Join the rows. Press seams in one direction. Sew a green dot I triangle to each angled corner to complete the 34½" x 34½" quilt center. Press seams toward the triangles.

3. Trim the 2½" x 42" medium blue print strips to make two 34½" strips and two 38½" strips. Sew the shorter strips to opposite sides and the longer strips to the remaining sides of the quilt center. Press seams toward the strips. *Note: Refer to Finishing Basics on page 26 for information about cutting border strips.*

4. Trim the 1½" x 42" white print strips to make two 38½" strips and two 40½" strips. Sew the shorter strips to opposite sides and the longer strips to the remaining sides of the quilt center. Press seams toward the strips.

5. Trim two 4½" x 42" navy floral strips to make two 40½" strips. Sew these strips to opposite sides of the quilt center. Sew the remaining 4½" x 42" navy floral strips short ends together to make a long strip. Press seams to one side. Cut into two 48½" strips. Sew the strips to the remaining sides to complete the quilt top. Press seams toward the strips.

FINISHING THE QUILT

1. Remove the selvage edges from the backing pieces. Sew the pieces together down the length with a ½" seam allowance. Trim the sides to make a 56" x 56" backing piece. Press seam open.

2. Refer to Finishing Basics to layer, quilt, and bind your quilt.

Build It Better

Don't let diagonal rows make you dizzy! Mark the row numbers on small pieces of paper and pin them to the top piece in each row. It's a snap to keep track of the layout and the order of the blocks in the rows.

Quilt Assembly Diagram

The stars really stand out on the light, plain background of this version of *Dressed to the Nines*. This quilt is a perfect size for a new mom to use as a play mat for baby. A great take-along in the stroller or car for those unexpected stops at the park!

Scene Through a Telescope

Whole families of stars populate the center of this bed-size quilt. Half-size blocks make perfect size and style setting squares to complement the large star blocks. The colors and shapes of the small blocks echo those of the large blocks, while leaving lots of subdued background to offset the busyness of the diagonal stripe setting triangles.

Finished Quilt Size: 88" x 110$^1/_2$"
Finished Block Size: 16" x 16" and 8" x 8"
Number of Blocks: 12 and 12
Skill Level: Confident Beginner

MATERIALS
All yardages are based on 42"-wide fabric.

❖ $^7/_8$ yard of large circle print
❖ 2$^1/_4$ yards of diagonal stripe
❖ 3$^1/_4$ yards of white/gray print
❖ 3$^1/_2$ yards of red/black print
❖ 2$^7/_8$ yards of black floral
❖ 10$^1/_8$ yards of backing fabric
❖ 96" x 119" piece of batting
❖ Thread to match fabrics
❖ Rotary cutting tools
❖ Basic sewing supplies

CUTTING

Label all pieces with the letters assigned. They will be used throughout the instructions. All pieces labeled with a letter and 1 are for the large blocks; those labeled with a letter and 2 are for the small blocks.

From the large circle print, cut
- 3 strips 8$\frac{1}{2}$" x 42"; recut into (12) 8$\frac{1}{2}$" A1 squares

From the diagonal stripe, cut
- 3 strips 23$\frac{7}{8}$" x 42"; recut into (3) 23$\frac{7}{8}$" F squares, (2) 12$\frac{1}{4}$" G squares, and (12) 4$\frac{1}{2}$" A2 squares, then cut the F squares twice diagonally to make 12 F triangles and the G squares in half diagonally to make 4 G triangles

From the white/gray print, cut
- 18 strips 4$\frac{1}{2}$" x 42"; recut into (48) 4$\frac{1}{2}$" x 8$\frac{1}{2}$" B1 rectangles and (48) 4$\frac{1}{2}$" D1 squares
- 9 strips 2$\frac{1}{2}$" x 42"; recut into (48) 2$\frac{1}{2}$" x 4$\frac{1}{2}$" B2 rectangles and (48) 2$\frac{1}{2}$" D2 squares

From the red/black print, cut
- 11 strips 4$\frac{1}{2}$" x 42"; recut into (96) 4$\frac{1}{2}$" C1 squares
- 6 strips 2$\frac{1}{2}$" x 42"; recut into (96) 2$\frac{1}{2}$" C2 squares
- 8 strips 3$\frac{1}{2}$" x 42" for inner border
- 10 strips 2$\frac{1}{4}$" x 42" for binding

From the black floral, cut
- 3 strips 8$\frac{1}{2}$" x 42"; recut into (12) 8$\frac{1}{2}$" E squares
- 9 strips 7$\frac{1}{2}$" x 42" for outer border

From the backing fabric, cut
- 3 pieces 119" long

MAKING THE SAWTOOTH STAR BLOCKS

Use a $\frac{1}{4}$" seam allowance throughout unless otherwise instructed.

1. Refer to Building the Block on page 6 to make (12) 16$\frac{1}{2}$" x 16$\frac{1}{2}$" large Sawtooth Star blocks, using the A1—D1 pieces.

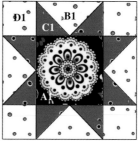

Make 12

2. Refer to Building the Block on page 6 to make (12) 8$\frac{1}{2}$" x 8$\frac{1}{2}$" small Sawtooth Star blocks, using the A2—D2 pieces.

Make 12

3. Sew a black floral E square to one side of a small block to make a row. Press seams toward the E square. Repeat to make a second row. Sew the rows together to complete one setting square. Press seam in one direction. Repeat to make six setting squares total.

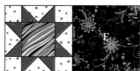

Make 6

COMPLETING THE TOP

1. Join the large blocks, setting squares, and diagonal stripe F triangles in six diagonal rows. Press seams in each row away from the large blocks. There will be two leftover F triangles. (See the Quilt Assembly Diagram on page 18.)

2. Join the rows. Press seams in one direction. Sew a diagonal stripe G triangle to each angled corner to complete the 68½" x 91" quilt center. Press seams toward the triangles.

3. Sew the 3½" x 42" red/black print strips short ends together to make a long strip. Press seams to one side. Cut into two 91" strips and two 74½" strips. Sew the longer strips to the long sides and the shorter strips to the top and bottom of the quilt center. Press seams toward the strips. *Note: Refer to Finishing Basics on page 26 for information about cutting border strips.*

4. Sew the 7½" x 42" black floral strips short ends together to make a long strip. Press seams to one side. Cut into two 97" strips and two 88½" strips. Sew the longer strips to the long sides and the shorter strips to the top and bottom to complete the quilt top. Press seams toward the strips.

FINISHING THE QUILT

1. Remove the selvage edges from the backing pieces. Sew the pieces together down the length with a ½" seam allowance. Trim the sides to make a 96" x 119" backing piece. Press seams open.

2. Refer to Finishing Basics to layer, quilt, and bind your quilt.

Build It Better

Using a straight or diagonal stripe for setting triangles adds lots of interest and movement, but make sure to plan ahead. The side and top/bottom triangles are from a square that is cut twice diagonally. The stripe will run in one direction on two of the triangles from one square and in the other direction on the other two triangles. The corner triangles are from a square that is cut in half diagonally. The direction of your cut makes a difference in the way the stripe will be placed in your quilt.

All of these changes in direction can have a big impact on the design of your quilt. Wait to cut the corner triangles until you can preview them in your quilt. Lay out the blocks with the side and top/bottom triangles, then fold the corner triangles in half diagonally and place them in the layout to plan the direction of the stripe.

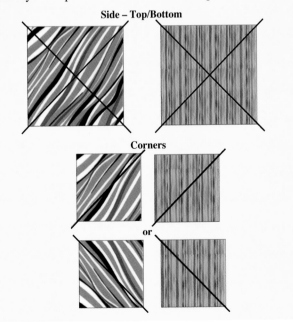

Side – Top/Bottom

Corners

or

Quilt Assembly Diagram

Black is often the go-to color for accent. In this case, rust star points dull the effect of the rich autumn colors, while green star points disappear into the background. Black is often used to "pop" the colors in a fabric (as seen in the autumn prints of this quilt). It has the same use when placed in pieces of a quilt.

Framed Stars

Sawtooth Star blocks are set with sashing frames in this soft, feminine quilt. Instructions are given for unpieced borders for the beginner quilter and pieced borders for the intermediate quilter.

Finished Quilt Size: 64" x 79"
Finished Block Size: 12" x 12"
Number of Blocks: 12
Skill Level: Beginner/Intermediate

MATERIALS

All yardages are based on 42"-wide fabric.

- ❖ 1 3/4 yards of large pink floral
- ❖ 3/4 yard of light pink print
- ❖ 1 1/4 yards of light gray print
- ❖ 2 yards of black print
- ❖ 1 1/8 yards of gray/pink dot
- ❖ 7/8 yard of small pink floral (pieced border) or 1/4 yard (unpieced border)
- ❖ 5 yards of backing fabric
- ❖ 72" x 87" piece of batting
- ❖ Thread to match fabrics
- ❖ Template material
- ❖ Rotary cutting tools
- ❖ Basic sewing supplies

CUTTING

Label all pieces with the letters assigned. They will be used throughout the instructions. All pieces labeled with a letter and 1 are for the pink blocks; those labeled with a letter and 2 are for the gray blocks.

From the large pink floral, cut
- 2 strips 6 1/2" x 42"; recut into (12) 6 1/2" A squares
- 7 strips 6 1/2" x 42" for outer border

From the light pink print, cut
- 6 strips 3 1/2" x 42"; recut into (24) 3 1/2" x 6 1/2" B1 rectangles and (24) 3 1/2" D1 squares

From the light gray print, cut
- 6 strips 3 1/2" x 42"; recut into (24) 3 1/2" x 6 1/2" B2 rectangles and (24) 3 1/2" D2 squares

From the black print, cut
- 8 strips 3 1/2" x 42"; recut into (96) 3 1/2" C squares
- 8 strips 2 1/4" x 42" for binding

From the gray/pink dot, cut
- 6 strips 2 1/2" x 42"; recut into (17) 2 1/2" x 12 1/2" E strips
- 3 strips 2 5/8" x 42" for inner border
- 3 strips 3" x 42" for inner border

From the small pink floral, cut
- 1 strip 2 1/2" x 42"; recut into (6) 2 1/2" F squares

From the backing fabric, cut
- 2 pieces 87" long

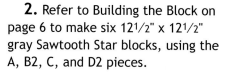

ADDITIONAL CUTTING

Instructions are given for pieced borders for the intermediate quilter and unpieced borders for the beginning quilter. The following is the cutting information for the borders.

1. For the pieced borders, make full-size templates for the G, H, and I/J pieces (given on page 24) by tracing each half-template onto a large piece of paper. Fold the paper on the dashed fold line of the template. Cut out the template through both layers. *Note: The J template is made by placing the inside dashed line of the I template on the fold of a sheet of paper.*

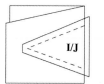

2. Cut 14 G pieces from the small pink floral, 28 H pieces from the light gray print, and 8 I pieces and 10 J pieces from the black print.

3. Cut 1 strip 4^1/^{2}" x 42" from the light gray print; recut into (4) 4^1/^{2}" K squares.

4. For the unpieced borders, cut 6 strips 2" x 42" from the light gray print and 6 strips 3" x 42" from the black print.

MAKING THE SAWTOOTH STAR BLOCKS

Use a ^{1}/^{4}" seam allowance throughout unless otherwise instructed.

1. Refer to Building the Block on page 6 to make six 12^1/^{2}" x 12^1/^{2}" pink Sawtooth Star blocks, using the A, B1, C, and D1 pieces.

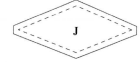

Make 6

2. Refer to Building the Block on page 6 to make six 12^1/^{2}" x 12^1/^{2}" gray Sawtooth Star blocks, using the A, B2, C, and D2 pieces.

Make 6

COMPLETING THE QUILT CENTER

1. Sew two pink blocks and one gray block alternately together with two gray/pink E strips to make an A row. Press seams toward the E strips. Repeat to make a second A row.

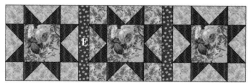

A Row – Make 2

2. Stitch two gray blocks and one pink block alternately together with two gray/pink E strips to make a B row. Press seams toward the E strips. Repeat to make a second B row.

B Row – Make 2

3. Sew three gray/pink E strips alternately together with two small pink floral F squares to make a sashing row. Press seams toward the E strips. Repeat to make three sashing rows total.

Make 3

4. Stitch the A and B rows alternately together with the sashing rows to complete the 40^1/^{2}" x 54^1/^{2}" quilt center. Press seams toward the sashing rows. (See the Quilt Assembly Diagram on page 24.)

5. Sew the 2⅝" x 42" gray/pink strips short ends together to make a long strip. Press seams to one side. Cut into two 54½" strips. Sew the strips to the long sides of the quilt center. Press seams toward the strips. *Note: Refer to the Finishing Basics on page 26 for information about cutting border strips.*

6. Repeat step 5 with the 3" x 42" gray/pink strips and cut two 44¾" strips. Sew the strips to the top and bottom of the quilt center. Press seams toward the strips.

ADDING THE UNPIECED BORDERS

1. Sew the 2" x 42" light gray print strips short ends together to make a long strip. Press seams to one side. Cut into two 59½" strips and two 47¾" strips. Sew the longer strips to the long sides and the shorter strips to the top and bottom of the quilt center. Press seams toward the strips.

2. Stitch the 3" x 42" black print strips short ends together to make a long strip. Press seams to one side. Cut into two 62½" strips and two 52¾" strips. Sew the longer strips to the long sides and the shorter strips to the top and bottom of the quilt center. Press seams toward the strips.

3. Sew the 6½" x 42" large pink floral strips short ends together to make a long strip. Press seams to one side. Cut into two 67½" strips and two 64¾" strips. Sew the longer strips to the long sides and the shorter strips to the top and bottom to complete the quilt top. Press seams toward the strips.

4. Continue with Finishing the Quilt.

ADDING THE PIECED BORDERS

1. Sew a light gray H piece to two sides of each black J diamond to make 10 HJ units. Press seams toward the H pieces.

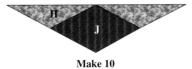

Make 10

2. Stitch a black I piece to one side of four light gray H pieces to make four HI units. Press seams toward the H pieces. Repeat to make four reversed HI units.

Make 4   Reversed
                Make 4

3. Sew four pink G pieces alternately together with three HJ units. Press seams toward the G pieces. Sew an HI unit to one end and a reversed HI unit to the remaining end to complete one side border strip. Press seams toward the G pieces. Repeat to make a second side border strip.

Side – Make 2

4. Sew the side border strips to the long sides of the quilt center. Press seams toward the gray/pink dot border.

5. Stitch three G pieces alternately together with two HJ units. Press seams toward the G pieces. Sew an HI unit to one end and a reversed HI unit to the remaining end. Press seams toward the G pieces. Sew a light gray K square to each end of the strip. Press seams toward the K squares to complete the top border strip. Repeat to make the bottom border strip.

Top/Bottom – Make 2

6. Sew the pieced strips to the top and bottom of the quilt center. Press seams toward the gray/pink dot border.

7. Repeat steps 3 and 4 of Adding the Unpieced Borders to complete the quilt top.

FINISHING THE QUILT

1. Remove the selvage edges from the backing pieces. Sew the pieces together down the length with a ½" seam allowance. Trim the sides to make a 72" x 87" backing piece. Press seam open.

2. Refer to Finishing Basics to layer, quilt, and bind your quilt.

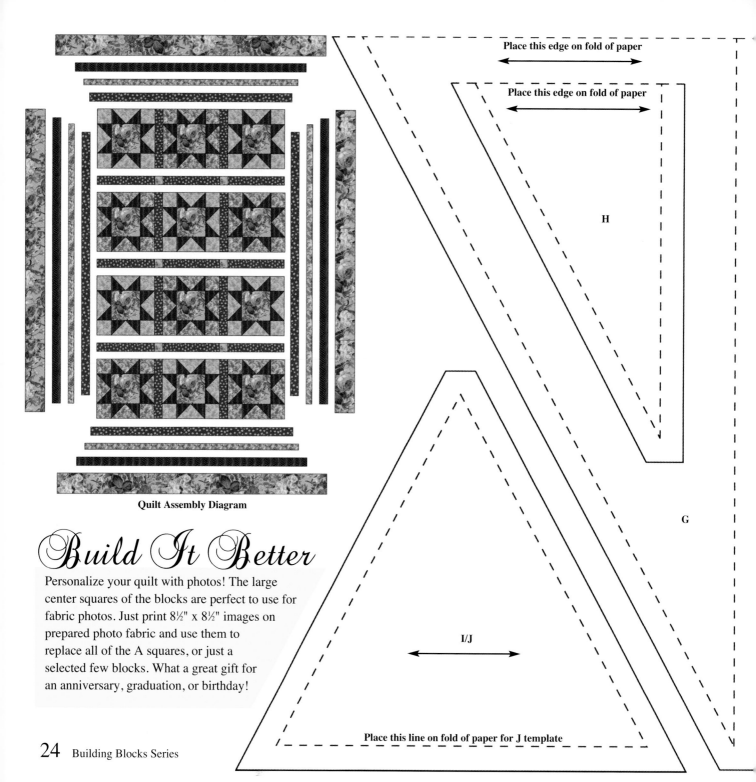

Quilt Assembly Diagram

Build It Better

Personalize your quilt with photos! The large center squares of the blocks are perfect to use for fabric photos. Just print 8½" x 8½" images on prepared photo fabric and use them to replace all of the A squares, or just a selected few blocks. What a great gift for an anniversary, graduation, or birthday!

Place this edge on fold of paper

Place this edge on fold of paper

H

G

I/J

Place this line on fold of paper for J template

The large center squares of the blocks are just right for showcasing a special print.
In this quick-to-make child's quilt, the pages from a book panel fit perfectly.

Finishing Basics

ADDING BORDERS

Borders are an important part of your quilt. They add another design element, and act much like a picture frame to complement and support the center.

There are two basic types of borders—butted corners and mitered corners. Butted corners are the most common. For this technique, border strips are stitched to opposite sides of the quilt center, pressed, and then strips are sewn to the remaining sides. Mitered corners are often used to continue a pattern around the corners; for example, the stripe in a fabric or a pieced border design.

Butted corners   **Mitered corners**

Lengths are given for the borders in the individual quilt instructions. In most cases, fabric-width strips are joined to make a strip long enough to cut two side strips and top and bottom strips. Because of differences in piecing and pressing, your quilt center may differ slightly in size from the mathematically exact

size used to determine the border lengths. Before cutting the strips for butted corners, refer to the instructions given here to measure for lengths to fit your quilt center. For mitered borders, extra length is already included in the sizes given in the instructions to make it easier to stitch the miters. It should be enough to allow for any overall size differences.

BUTTED CORNERS

1. Press the quilt center. Arrange it on a flat surface with the edges straight.

2. Fold the quilt in half lengthwise, matching edges and corners. Finger-press the center fold to make a crease. Unfold.

3. Measure along the center ceased line to determine the length of the quilt center.

 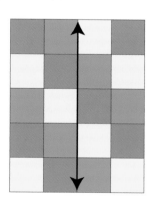

Fold in half

4. Cut two strips this length.

5. Fold the strips in half across the width and finger-press to make a crease.

6. Place a strip right sides together on one long edge of the quilt center, aligning the creased center of the strip with the center of the long edge. Pin in place at the center. Align the ends of the strips with the top and bottom edges of the quilt center. Pin in place at each end.

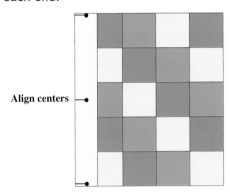

Align centers

7. Pin between the ends and center, easing any full-ness, if necessary.

8. Stitch the border to the quilt center. Press.

9. Repeat on the remaining long edge.

10. Fold the quilt in half across the width and crease to mark the center. Unfold. Measure along the creased line to determine the width of the bordered quilt center.

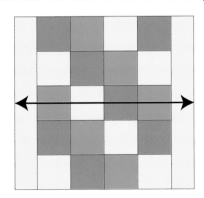

11. Cut two strips this length.

12. Repeat steps 5—9 on the top and bottom edges of the quilt center.

MITERED CORNERS

1. Prepare the border strips as directed in the individual pattern.

2. Make a mark 1/4" on each side of the quilt corners.

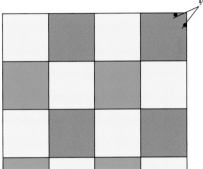

3. Center the border strips on each side of the quilt top and pin in place. Stitch in place, stopping and lock-ing stitches at the 1/4" mark at each corner.

4. Fold the quilt top in half diagonally with wrong sides together. Arrange two border ends right sides together.

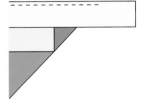

5. Mark a 45° angle line from the locked stitching on the border to the outside edge of the border.

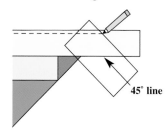

45° line

6. Stitch on the marked line, starting exactly at the locked stitch. Trim seam allowance to 1/4".

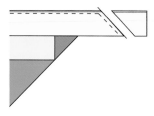

7. Press the mitered corner seam open and the seam between the border and the rest of the quilt toward the border.

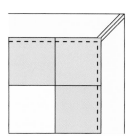

8. Repeat these steps on each corner of the quilt.

LAYERING, BASTING & QUILTING

You may choose to do your own quilting or take your projects to a machine quilter. Be sure that your backing and batting are at least 4" wider and 4" longer on each side of the quilt top. The size needed is given in the Materials list for each project.

If you would like to quilt your own project, there are many good books about hand and machine quilting. Check with your quilting friends or at your local quilt shop for recommendations. Here are the basic steps to do your own quilting:

1. Mark the quilt top with a quilting design, if desired.

2. Place the backing right side down on a flat surface. Place the batting on top. Center the quilt top right side up on top of the batting. Smooth all the layers. Thread-baste, pin, or spray-baste the layers together to hold while quilting.

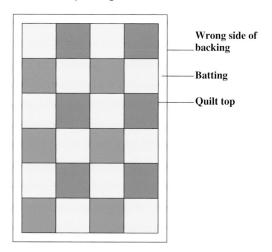

Wrong side of backing

Batting

Quilt top

3. Quilt the layers by hand or machine.
4. When quilting is finished, trim the batting and backing even with the quilted top.

BINDING

The patterns in this book include plenty of fabric to cut either 2¼" or 2½" wide strips for straight-grain, double-fold binding. In some cases, a wider binding or bias binding is needed because of a specific edge treatment; extra yardage is included when necessary.

PREPARING STRAIGHT-GRAIN, DOUBLE-FOLD BINDING

1. Cut strips as directed for the individual pattern. Remove selvage edges.

2. Place the ends of two binding strips right sides together at a right angle. Mark a line from inside corner to inside corner. Stitch on the marked line. Trim seam allowance to ¼".

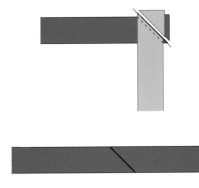

3. Repeat step 2 to join all binding strips into one long strip. Press seams to one side. Fold the strip in half lengthwise with wrong sides together and press.

PREPARING DOUBLE-FOLD BIAS BINDING

1. Cut an 18" x 42" strip from the binding fabric.

2. Place the 45° angle line of a rotary ruler on one edge of the strip. Trim off one corner of the strip.

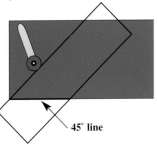

45° line

3. Cut binding strips in the width specified in the pattern from the angled end of the strip.

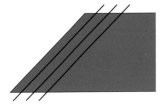

4. Each strip will be approximately 25" long. Cut strips to total the length needed for the pattern, repeating steps 1 and 2 if needed.

5. Align the ends of two strips with right sides together. Stitch ¼" from the ends.

6. Repeat to join all binding strips into one long strip. Press seams to one side.

ADDING THE BINDING

1. Leaving a 6"-8" tail and beginning several inches from a corner, align the raw edges of the binding with the edge of the quilt. Stitch along the edge with a $1/4$" seam allowance, locking stitches at the beginning.

2. Stop $1/4$" from the first corner and lock stitching. Remove the quilt from your machine. Turn the quilt so the next edge is to your right. Fold the binding end up and then back down so the fold is aligned with the previous edge of the quilt and the binding is aligned with the edge to your right. Starting at the edge of the quilt, stitch the binding to the next corner.

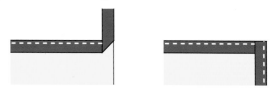

3. Repeat step 2 to attach binding to the rest of the quilt, stopping stitching 6"–8" from the starting point and locking stitches.

4. Unfold the ends of the strips. Press flat. About halfway between the stitched ends, fold the beginning strip up at a right angle. Press. Fold the ending strip down at a right angle, with the folded edge butted against the fold of the beginning end. Press.

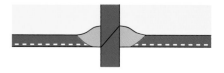

5. Trim each end $1/4$" from creased fold. Place the trimmed ends right sides together. Pin to hold. Stitch $1/4$" from the ends. Press the seam allowance open.

6. Refold the strip in half. Press. Arrange the strip on the edge of the quilt and stitch in place to finish the binding.

7. Fold the edge of the binding over the raw edges to the back of the quilt. Hand stitch in place, covering the machine stitches and mitering the corners.

COLLECT THEM ALL! Look for the complete Building Blocks Series 1 Books 1–8 at your local quilt shop, favorite book store, or order www.allamericancrafts.com.

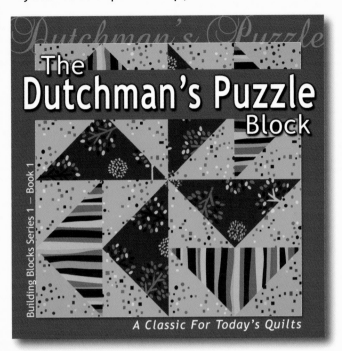

The **Dutchman's Puzzle** Block

Building Blocks Series 1 — Book 1

A Classic For Today's Quilts

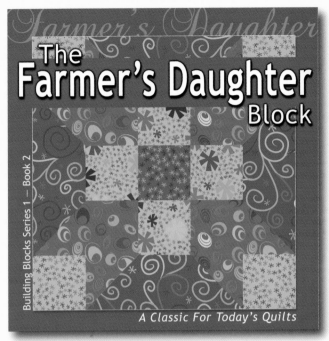

The **Farmer's Daughter** Block

Building Blocks Series 1 — Book 2

A Classic For Today's Quilts

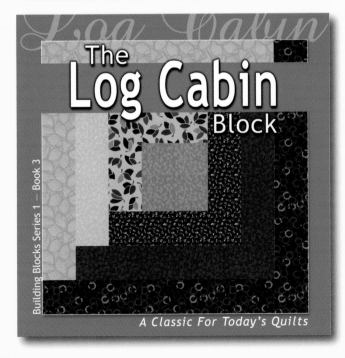

The **Log Cabin** Block

Building Blocks Series 1 — Book 3

A Classic For Today's Quilts

The **Snail's Trail** Block

Building Blocks Series 1 — Book 4

A Classic For Today's Quilts

Books 5-8 →

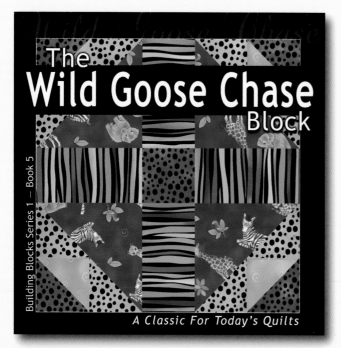

The **Wild Goose Chase** Block

Building Blocks Series 1 – Book 5

A Classic For Today's Quilts

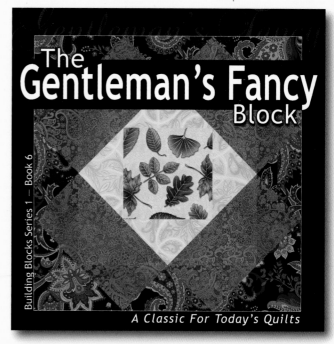

The **Gentleman's Fancy** Block

Building Blocks Series 1 – Book 6

A Classic For Today's Quilts

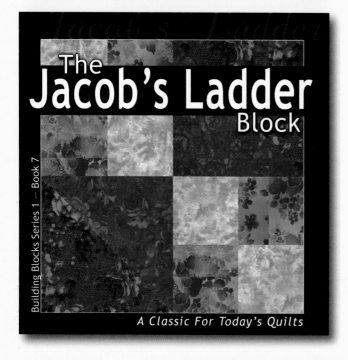

The **Jacob's Ladder** Block

Building Blocks Series 1 – Book 7

A Classic For Today's Quilts

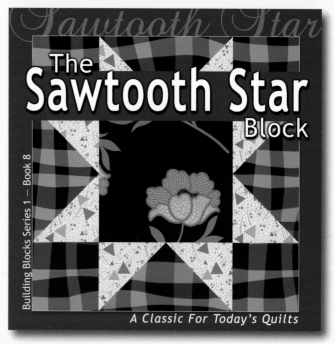

The **Sawtooth Star** Block

Building Blocks Series 1 – Book 8

A Classic For Today's Quilts